YESTERDAYS

Published by: A3TCO
PO Box 9181
Salem OR 97305

Cover Design and Artwork by Sheila Somerville. The artist may be contacted by writing to A3TCO.

ISBN: 1-884366-05-8

Other books in the Uncle Bud series:

I Remember When
SweetMemories
Lookin' Back
Reflections
What's Cookin'?

I'd hate to disappoint you, so if you're sitting in with our morning group and the term "getting a little action" comes up, what you're about to hear is a discussion on the merits of the various forms of fiber.

"Marge is a good cook," says Joe, "but like everybody she had to learn. One fall, right after we were married, she made biscuits. And to say they were 'heavy' would be a real understatement. To her credit she admitted it and put 'em out for the birds to eat. I'd never have let her do it if I'd thought the birds would actually eat 'em. But they did. One of my regrets in life."

"How's that?" asks Pete.

"Well," says Joe as he sips his coffee, "It's pitiful to see birds walkin' south for the winter. Just pitiful."

"A man gets smarter once he's married," Luther observed. As everyone around the table nodded in agreement, Luther went on, "'Course by then, it's too late."

"You know you've reached a certain point in life," says Pete, "when you wake up in the night and find your wife's face about a foot above yours. And you say ..."

"What?"

"I thought you were dead."

"Well, I'm not."

"I thought you were."

"And have you cash in that insurance policy while you're still young enough to enjoy it. Not a chance."

When Pete and me went fishin' the other day he was telling me how he was at Luther's place givin' him a hand last spring. They were digging thistles out of the alfalfa field. At the time they were in a corner of the field next to the road and just across the fence from the cow pasture.

Just then a car came along, slowed, and pulled over. A man got out and crawled through the fence into the pasture practically in front of Luther and Pete. There's a low spot in that corner of the pasture, and a bunch of what Luther took to be toadstools but what this fella had evidently identified as mushrooms. Anyhow, the guy goes to pullin' 'em up and dropping 'em into a paper sack. Just then he notices ol' Beauregard.

Now you may recall that Beauregard is Luther's Holstein bull. As far as his size goes, just try to picture a box car with horns. And if Luther ain't fond of havin' people crawl through his fences and pick his toadstools or whatever, ol'

2

Beauregard is downright hostile about it.

About then this fella notices the bull who has also noticed him. He looks over at Luther and says, "Hey! Is that bull safe?"

Luther leans on his shovel and replies, "Oh, he's safe enough."

The guy bends over and goes back to grabbin' mushrooms. Behind him ol' Beauregard is actin' as if somebody just spit in his julep and is sending a few dozen earthworms airborne.

"Can't say the same for you, though."

Tom's son called him from college recently and spent quite a while talkin' to him about what it was like to be married so long to the same woman. Naturally, Tom got a little suspicious and wanted to know what this was all about.

"I've got a part in the school play," says Herb. "My role is that of a man who's been married for thirty years."

"Well, keep trying," says Tom. "Maybe next time you'll get a speaking part."

Doc Guthrie stopped by for coffee the other morning. "When I was in the Army," she said, "a man was brought to the hospital by his wife. I checked him over and then went out to the waiting room to talk to her. *I don't like the looks of your husband,* I said."

"The wife shook her head. *Neither do I,* she replied, *but he is good with the children.*"

Have you ever heard some broadcaster refer to a politician as a "favorite son"? Ever wonder if he just forgot to finish the sentence?

"The problem with sittin' around doing nothin'," says Joe, "is you can never be absolutely sure when you're finished."

Frank Peagram, you remember, was a good carpenter, but ol' Frank did like to pull a cork. Now, Mabel Fitch knew about Frank's habits like everybody else around here, but when she hired Frank to build a small addition on her house, things changed. Mabel, you see, was a teetotaler and decided that while Frank was working for her that he would be, too.

One day she really ripped into ol' Frank. "I saw that old pickup of yours parked outside of Jensen's Tavern," she said. "I won't have the local people thinking that I permit drunkards to be in my employ." She turned around and stomped off.

Frank didn't say a word. He just left his old

pickup parked in front of Mabel's house. All night.

"It seems odd to me," Joe was sayin', "That the words 'capitol' and 'capital' mean two completely different things. And yet you can say that the Capitol of the United States is in Washington, D.C."

He took a drink of coffee and shook his head. "And you can also say that the capital of the United States is in Washington, D.C."

Hey, here's the latest in the gopher and mole wars. Now, let's say you don't wanna croak this poor gopher that's makin' your yard look like a plowed field. Even better, let's say you've got a neighbor you don't much like. Well, I hear gophers don't like the smell of moth balls any more than skunks do ... so they pack their little bags and move on ... hopefully over to the neighbors.

Moles, it seems, feel the same way about castor oil. You spray it on at an ounce to the gallon of water. Use one of those hose-end sprayers that lets you put full strength stuff in the cup and you use the dial to set the mix rate. Be sure to water heavily after you've put it down.

Moles, by the way, show up when you've got

obnoxious critters in your lawn. They're after grubs, usually, and these come from crickets that figure whatever you like to grow must be good to eat. There are various concoctions you can buy at the yard and garden store to bump off these little varmints. No crickets ... no grubs ... no moles.

"I was channel surfin' last night," Tom was saying, "and I came across one of those dopey horror movies. There's this woman, right? Now, let's say she wants to do the laundry. She opens the basement door, turns on the light, and goes downstairs to do the job.

"Only now it's midnight. She's alone in the house. On the news they're telling everyone that there's a homicidal maniac running loose in the neighborhood.

"She hears a noise in the basement. What does she do? Lock and barricade the basement door? Call the cops? Not a chance. She eases the basement door open (which has suddenly developed a creaking noise) and, shaking with fear, passes the light switch on her way down the stairs.

"Each stair step has caught the creaking disease from the door, and they announce her every movement to the ax murderer below. Apparently, she thinks the fiend won't be able to find her in the dark, so she searches the whole place. She knocks over boxes and bicycles and steps on the cat's tail. She is practically fainting from fear every time she blunders into something. Finally, she decides the noise was only the cat and, with great relief, starts back upstairs.

"It's then that the killer wakes up from his nap or coma or finishes his sandwich or whatever and grabs her. Then he proceeds to slice, dice, chop and shred her into a blob of goo."

Tom takes a swig of coffee. "Good thing, too. After all this time I was ready to murder the idiot myself."

Bill Larson, our local county mountie, was in the other morning. Now, I'm not sayin' ol' Bill would stretch a story so you'll just have to decide for yourself.

"I'm sittin' in the sheriff's office not long ago," Bill says, "when this man walks in."

"*I've just shot a politician*, the guy tells me."

"*Down the hall, third door on the left*," I say, nodding at the hallway. "*That's the game warden's office. You collect your bounty there*."

Gladys was telling Pete about their new neighbors. "For their anniversary," Gladys said, "he took her to dinner and a movie. Then they spent the night in a hotel. That's so romantic.

Why don't you do something like that?"

"Well, I might," nodded Pete. "But I'd want to get a good look at her first."

There are still a few among us who remember when gasoline sold for fifteen or twenty cents a gallon. There are fewer still who recall they were working for a buck an hour at the time.

"I went huntin' up in that north country last fall," Luther was sayin'. "I'm not familiar with that neck o' the woods, and I hate to admit it, but I got lost.

"I'm wanderin' around out there, and it's gettin' dark. Just when I think I'm gonna have to spend the night out in the boondocks, I spot a building. I finally break out of the brush and get a closer look.

"By golly, it's a monastery! The monks tell me where I am and, since it's that time, invite me in for supper. Well, it's fish and chips, and just about the finest I ever threwed a lip over. I was mighty hungry after the day I'd had, so after my third big helping, I lean back, give a big sigh and look at all those monks sittin' at that long table.

"*Man, that was good!* I say to nobody in particular."

"*Thank you*, says the fella sittin' next to me.

It's nice to be appreciated."

"Did you make supper? I asked."

"Not all of it, he says. *I'm the fish friar,* and he points to the guy across the table. *He's the chip monk."*

Pete darn near choked on his coffee.

Martha is a little worried about what the critics will say about the book she's written. I told her to take a day and go tour the state capitol. "You'll find a lot of statues of men and women who devoted their lives to one thing or another," I said. "Let me know if you find one that says *CRITIC.*"

Janie, as you may recall, was kind of an afterthought in Tom and Alice's family plans. With her brothers being eight and twelve years older, Janie turned into something of a tomboy. By the time she was ten, she looked on the world in much the same way as her teenage brother.

Anyhow, according to Tom, they had a neighbor lady who had a big ol' tomcat. (Gettin' hard to keep track of all the "Toms," ain't it?) Now this tomcat had decided that Tom and Alice's patio belonged to him and kept it well "irrigated" to advertise his ownership. Complaining to the neighbor did no good.

You've got to let a cat be a cat, she'd say.

"Well," Tom went on, "Janie had a pet parakeet, and she'd take him out on the patio and let him fly around and sit on her shoulder. One day the phone rang and she ran to answer it, leaving the bird outside. Twenty minutes later the neighbor lady is leaning on the fence watching Janie fill in a hole she'd dug with a shovel."

Whatever are you doing, there, Janie? the lady asked.

It's a grave for my parakeet, Janie replies.

My, that's a large grave for a parakeet.

Had to be, says Janie, *because he's inside your damned ol' cat.*

Zeke claims one good thing about getting old and forgetful is he's always meeting new people.

"I don't know who is responsible for all this violence on television," says Pete, "but we oughta hunt him up an beat the hell out of him."

"It's sound advice," says Joe, "to walk a mile in someone's shoes before you criticize. You're always better off bein' a mile away from somebody who wants to punch your lights out, and especially so if they're barefooted."

LeRoy does come in and cage a free burger once in a while, and he hits other folks up for handouts sometimes. But since he doesn't make a habit of it, nobody complains too much. The other day, though, he asked Tom for twenty-five bucks.

"Twenty-five dollars?" yells Tom. "You can get the best meal in town for half that amount."

LeRoy puffs up and looks at Tom like he's simple. "I know that," he says, "I have a date."

One Easter some town folks bought three little yellow balls of fluff that just looked so cute paddlin' around in the kids' wading pool. Then they started to grow. The neighbors weren't real fond of having three noisy geese next door, and that's how they came to be on our place.

Outside of a dog, cat, or horse, you won't find pets on a working farm or ranch. You don't want to get too friendly with a critter that just might wind up as the main course for supper. But these geese were given to Mom by friends and were, therefore, pets.

Now, the two geese were okay, but the gander, he was a different story. Gus, as he came to be called, kept getting bigger ... and meaner, every day. Ever been flogged by a big ol' ornery gander? Not only does it hurt, but for a kid it's pretty scary.

Something had to be done. Our BB guns were

useless on a critter this size, so my brother and I came up with a plan. We organized a lynch mob of two and set up an ambush for ol' Gus. A gander though is pretty alert and suspicious, so the ambushers got ambushed and chased to the house a half dozen times. Finally, using some grain as bait, we managed to drop a loop on him. We both held the rope, ran like crazy for the nearest tree and tossed the loose end over a limb. We were just stringing him up when Mom caught us, turned him loose and gave us a good tongue-lashing. Gus, to give the devil his due, had the good sense not to attack Mom.

He did have a trick, though, that he reserved for adults. He'd sneak up behind 'em, turn his head sideways and grab 'em on the back of the knee right at the top of the calf. Then he'd set his heels and pull until the skin snapped out of his bill. Now, if you were one of those people who dig their own pain, the best way to describe it would be - exquisite. Then he'd turn around and run. The victim, his eyes full of tears, couldn't have found his own hat at the moment, anyhow.

At first Gus reserved this little prank for visitors, but they became real scarce after a while, so he started in on Dad. Granted, he won the first few rounds and some dark threats were made, but Mom would have none of it. Gus had been a gift from friends. He was a pet, she said.

Now, I don't want to make ol' Gus out to be

worse than he really was. Lookin' back, I'd have to say that he was no better or worse than your average, garden variety homicidal maniac. It's just that it's tough for a kid to have to peek out the door and locate the problem before he dares to step outside. Well, one morning I peeked out and saw I could step outside. Dad was coming from the barn with a full bucket of milk in each hand. Gus was sneakin' up behind him. Sure, I could have yelled a warning, but I knew it wouldn't take much more to drive Dad over the edge. Gus nailed him.

Maybe it was seeing two buckets twenty feet in the air or the rainbows created by the sun shining through a mist of milk that made Gus slow to react. I doubt it was Dad's howl of pain 'cause Gus was used to that. Anyhow, Dad whirled around, grabbed, and caught a neck. Dad, you see, grew up when the only starter for a gasoline-powered vehicle was a crank and right then he demonstrated what the term "spinnin' the crank" really meant. After a half-minute or so of this, he finished up with an Olympic-caliber hammer throw that landed Gus in a heap thirty feet out in the pasture.

Mom immediately called a family meeting. In a two-to-one majority vote (with one abstention), it was agreed that a couple of buckets of milk and a nasty strawberry on dad's leg was a small price to pay for the freedom to go outside unmolested.

We adjourned from the kitchen to the back porch.

And there, down by the creek with his two ladies, stood Gus. Somehow I'd known it all along. Deep down I knew that nothing short of a silver bullet or stake through the heart would release us from his clutches. All this happened shortly after Halloween.

As I recall, it was a couple of weeks later and Mom was hanging out the wash when Gus made a fatal error in judgment. That big strawberry on the back of Mom's knee had turned to a lovely purple edged with yellow by Thanksgiving morning. I remember it as she bent over the open oven and basted Ol' Gus. Later that day, Gus (now a nice golden brown) joined us for dinner. And I'm here to tell you, brother, you couldn't stick a fork in the gravy.

Mom decided he needed more time. Well he wasn't in the hot place I had envisioned him for so long, but it would do nicely. An hour later he was tougher yet, and an hour after that he was probably bulletproof.

Sometimes we tend to forget what Thanksgiving is really all about. I don't believe I've ever eaten such tasty pork chops.

A conversation you can count on having during the first ten miles of any trip:

"Did you turn off the coffee pot?"

"No ... Did you?"

Hey, y'know these tubes of adhesive and sealant and whatnot that you buy? Let's use silicone sealant as an example. You buy a tube of the stuff, use a little of it, then screw the cap back on and toss it in a drawer. Three months later, when you go to use it again, it's rock solid.

Well, get yourself a screw-top container that's big enough to hold those tubes of stuff. I use a plastic container that's wide enough to get my hand inside. Drop the tubes in, cap first, and fill the container about three-quarters full of water. Screw on the cap and you're done. The water keeps air out of the tubes, and the material inside won't set up or dry out. I've been doing this for over a year now, and the stuff in the tubes is still good as new.

Elmer had to go see Doc Guthrie a while back.

"Well, Elmer," she said, "it's hard to say exactly what's wrong ... and it's because of all that booze."

Elmer stood up and lurched toward the door. "Okay," he said. "I'll come back when you're sober."

18

Doc Guthrie isn't one to take any guff from anybody and ol' Elmer had managed to get on her bad side. The next time he came in, she checked out his complaint and then folded her arms and leaned against the wall.

"Tell me, Elmer," she said, "have you ever had this before?"

"Yeah, I have," Elmer replied.

"Well," she smiled, "you have it again."

Lately, we've been talking about family albums. Nobody's brought one into the cafe, but I'm sure we all went home and pulled ours out for another look over the last week or two. A couple of days ago we were talking about when the kids were little and old dogs we had and the folks we knew that aren't around any more.

Of course, Luther's a bachelor, so he kind of got left out of the conversation. Okay, maybe things were startin' to get a little mushy, but anyhow Luther finally sat back and looked at us kind of pitiful -- like, as if maybe none of us had an elevator that went all the way to the top.

"You guys and your albums," he said with a snort. "I don't need nothin' like that to remind me of the good times I've had. Why just the other day I cleaned out my refrigerator. There was a chicken wing in there from the barbecue I threw last summer. Kind of petrified, but it sure brought back memories. There was half a sandwich from the time Uncle Wilber and I went smelt dippin' down on the river."

"Your Uncle Wilber's been dead three, four years now," Pete recalled.

"We sure had a good time," Luther went on. "And do you remember that time you all came out to my place? About sun up so we could get an early start bird huntin'. I cooked breakfast for ever'body."

We all nodded.

"Well," said Luther, "the last of the pancake batter was there. It was gettin' pretty hairy, but I could still make out what it was. Them was sure good times," he smiled.

We took the hint and started talkin' about fishin'. Well, we did until Tom kind of frowned and looked over at Luther.

"Say, do you recall how last year Luther invited us all out to his place for a fish fry? It was smelt as I recall, and ... uhh, Luther ...?"

"When I was just a kid," Joe was sayin', "I was told the secret of a long, happy life. If I'd only understood what I was bein' told, I'd be better off today."

Naturally we were all a little curious, and Joe didn't keep us in suspense.

"I was talking to an old man who'd spent a

good part of his life huntin' grizzly bears, and I asked him how he did it."

"Well," the old fella says, "there's only two rules in dealin' with dangerous game. The first is to always take along a partner."

"What's the second?" I asked him.

"Be damned sure you can outrun him."

"I had an Uncle Willy," said Pete, "who went to buckarooin' in that juniper country down in the southern part of the state. It's no secret that once you get there, it's a long hoot and a holler to the next place. Willy and his partner Luke was out workin' the range one day when they came on a bull all tangled up in barb wire. The outfit they worked for wasn't much on this pedigreed stuff, and Willy said that while this bull would go about a ton, he figgered about ten percent of that was made up of horns.

"Anyhow, they shake out their loops and head and heel this critter. Once he's stretched out and down, they go to work on him with wire cutters and cut the wire away. Ever'body knows that an old range bull isn't exactly brimmin' with good cheer at any time, and this one, after bein' tangled up for a couple of days and gouged and scratched ever' time he took a step, well, he was hottern' a wet wildcat in a pepper patch.

"Luke had just cut the last of the wire away

when Willy took his rope off the bull's horns. All they had to do was get on their horses, shake the heel loop loose and make a clean getaway. But just then, the bull gave a lunge, broke the hondo on the loop around his back feet and got up ... between Luke and Willy and their horses.

"Now that juniper country has a lot of corners and sharp edges, and just behind them fellers was a scrawny little juniper tree ten or fifteen feet tall. Twenty feet behind it was a kind of rock face about the same height. The land sloped on up to the top of the ridge from there.

"Well, Willy and Luke were in a fix, but Willy got to the tree first and crawled up into it, fightin' his way past the branches as best he could, gettin' pretty scratched and scraped in the process. The tree was bendin' and swayin' pretty good, and it was obvious to Luke that the tree had already reached its buckaroo capacity. He ran on past it, lookin' for a way up that rock wall with the bull bellerin' and snortin' and blowin' snot on Luke's heels. There was a hole there, four or five feet up the wall and runnin' back into the rock. It was only a couple of feet in diameter, but to a cow puncher with steam blowin' in under his shirt tail, it looked like the Grand Canyon. Luke dove in head first, and the bull came up short, rattlin' his horns against the rocks and makin' all kinds of promises in what Willy said sounded like gutter-style cow talk.

"Finally the bull got tired of that and went back to make sure Willy got the same message. Willy was still there because the horses, sensible critters that they are, had decided that they were tired of all these shenanigans and may as well go home. Now, this tree was just tall enough to keep the heels of Willy's boots a foot or so above the bull's horns. It was pretty limber and tippy to begin with, but with Willy thrashin' around, and the bull hornin' the trunk and limbs, it got worse. Willy held on though and after a while, the bull figgered he'd made his position clear and started to wander off.

"Luke popped out of his hole. Here came the bull, chargin' back, and the whole process was repeated. He'd just started to amble off, when Luke came out of the hole again. Here comes the bull again, rattlin' his horns around the hole and hookin' and rammin' the tree, just itchin' for a cowboy kabob.

"It was early spring, Willy said, and the wind was blowin' right off the snow higher up and cuttin' through his clothes to where he was about half froze. Just as the bull started away, Luke popped out of the hole again.

"*Luke*, yelled Willy, *get back in that hole and stay there until that bull is gone.*

"*Can't*, whispered Luke, just loud enough to be heard.

"*Why not?*

"Luke jerked his thumb over his shoulder. *There's a damn cougar in that hole.*"

"I'm walking down the street yesterday," says Tom, "when ol' LeRoy stops me and hits me up for a loan of twenty bucks. Now, I don't mind helping LeRoy out once in a while, but this twenty dollar business is a little expensive for my taste.

"Taking out my wallet and holding it so LeRoy can't see how much cash I've got, I say, *Why, sure LeRoy.*

"Then I frown and pull out a ten dollar bill. *Well*, I say, *look at that. I've only got ten dollars on me.*

"LeRoy takes the money and says, *That's perfect.*

"As he's walking away I say, *LeRoy, I agreed to loan you twenty but only had ten to give you. How is that perfect.?*

"LeRoy stops and turns around with a smile. *Well*, he says, *now you owe me ten bucks and I owe you ten. We're even.*"

The practice of good judgment often comes from the application of bad judgment.

There's a fella named Timpson who roams the country around here selling folks insurance. He's a nice enough guy, but he doesn't quite know how to take some of us old timers. For instance, the other mornin' we were all sittin' around having our coffee when Timpson walks in and comes over to talk to Luther.

You may recall that Luther was married for a year or so when he was a young man. But ever since he came to this country, and it's been a long stretch, he's lived out there on his farm all by his lonesome. He likes it that way, too, but I have to admit that he's come to look at things a little differently from most folks.

Anyhow, Timpson steps up to the table and says, "Luther, you're not having problems with your hearing are you?"

"No," says Luther, "why?"

"Well, I wanted to talk to you about upgrading your insurance and ..."

"You mean buyin' more so the premiums'll be higher."

"No, not necessarily, I just wanted ..."

"Yeah, right." Luther took a swallow of coffee and looked sour.

"Anyway, I tried to phone you several times, but couldn't get an answer. Finally, I drove out to your place and knocked on the door. I could see you sitting at the kitchen table reading the newspaper and having a cup of coffee. Your back was to me, but I knocked and knocked. I knocked so hard I shook the door, but you never turned around."

Luther put his cup down and settled back in his chair. Those old gray eyes of his turned kind of icy and one eyebrow slowly raised as he regarded his man like you or I might look at a bug.

"Listen, Timpson," he said slowly, "I own that phone. The door belongs to me. I'll answer either one of 'em whenever I damn well feel like it."

Timpson look startled. "But you can't ..."

"Oh, yeah?" Luther interrupted. "Hide and watch me."

Well, Timpson gave it up as a bad bet and went on his way. The rest of us just sat there and nodded. We know Luther and accept him the way he is - not that we have any choice. He is what he is, take it or leave it. Sometimes I wonder what's going to happen when Luther cashes in his chips. If he goes to heaven, I think the Lord might be able to do something with him. But if he goes the other way, I don't think I'd want any part of the kind of work the devil's got in front of him.

"Have you noticed," Tom said, "how many stores now carry exercise equipment? And how many different kinds of machines there are? You can get machines that let you lift weights or ride a bike or ski or row a boat. You can walk up stairs or you can just walk on the level. There's a machine for just about any exercise you can bring to mind."

He took a swig of coffee and shook his head. "After seein' all kinds of machines in all kinds of folks' homes, though, I've come to the conclusion that these machines all lack an important feature. They should come equipped with hooks and hangers since ninety percent of them wind up as coat racks anyhow."

A door has two sides. The right side and the side the cat's on.

"Back in the days before the automobile," says Pete, "there were places in the West where a man caught stealin' a horse could wind up several inches taller and a whole lot deader in short order."

"I had a great uncle, Sydney," Pete goes on, "an' ol' Syd was known to be a little careless about where his loop landed. Travelin' through one of the aforementioned places, Syd found himself in the county hoosegow, charged with horse theft. At the trial, Syd took the stand and the prosecutor went right after him.

"Did you or did you not steal that horse?" the

lawyer says.

"No, I did not," Syd replies.

"Do you have any idea what the penalty is for perjury?" yells the lawyer.

"No, I don't," says Syd, "but I'll bet it's a helluva lot better than the penalty for horse stealin'."

Well, we had a little excitement here not long ago. It all started when Charles McKay came back to town. When Charlie was a teenager, he moved in with a family named Hall who lived west of town. I went to high school with Charlie, and I can't say I cared for him a whole lot. He wasn't a thief, but he'd cheat on tests and take advantage of the system whenever he got the chance. And he looked down on those who didn't do the same.

Charlie always had a smirk on his face when he talked to me. He wasn't shy about lettin' me know that he thought people like me, the ones that follow the rules, were all fools. After high school, he went in the service, and I heard later that he'd become an officer.

About four months ago Charlie came into the cafe. After all those years, I still recognized him right off. The horn-rimmed glasses looked the same, but the black hair had gone salt and pepper with a pencil-thin mustache added to kind of set things off. He was wearin' a nifty gray suit and the same smirk I remembered from our high school days. He only stayed long enough to let me know he'd retired from the service and was now a "financial advisor."

Even back in high school, ol' Charles had a way with the ladies, so it wasn't long before he had four or five of our local widows as clients. One of 'em was Georgia Hall. A couple of times, when it looked like Charlie would get kicked out of school for things he'd pulled, Georgie would be right down there defendin' him. Georgie thought ol' Charles could do no wrong.

Now, Charlie had liked to tease the younger kids, and one of 'em was Georgia's nephew, Tim. Charlie rode Tim pretty hard, and Tim, small as he was, tried to fight, but Charlie just laughed and held him off with one hand. Later, Tim grew - to like six-five and two-forty, but by then Charlie was long gone. Later still, Tim went to work for the state. Investigator. Financial Fraud Division. About two months ago he heard about his Aunt Georgia's new "financial advisor."

It was maybe ten days later, and we were just cleanin' up after the lunch rush and gettin' ready to close for the day when ol' Charles came in with Catherine Fuller. Catherine's husband, Ray, died about the same time Fred Hall did, and Catherine was a good friend of Georgia's.

Anyhow, the place was empty except for them when Georgie and Tom walked in along with four other widow ladies. I heard Georgie say, "I'll handle this," and Tim peeled off and came over to the counter. The best way to describe the look on Tim's face is to tell you to think of a fox with feathers on his chin.

Now, Georgie ain't a small woman, and she's an old farm girl to boot. She walked up to the table and, as ol' Charles stood up, she brought a right hook from somewhere south of Laredo and pasted him right in the eye. He landed in a corner and while he was gettin' up, Georgie let the other women know what Tim had found out.

Of course, it was all a scam and before Charlie knew it, those women had him trapped in that corner. It was kind of a strange fight, because they'd yell for a half a minute, and then one of the women would haul off and wallop him up side the noggin'. Sometimes they weren't too careful about what they had in their hands at the time, and my stock of plates and glassware was beginnin' to suffer some.

Jean, my head waitress, didn't know Charles, and she was sayin', "*We should stop this*," and "*Oh, this is terrible*," and other stuff like that. But me 'n Tim was just leanin' on the counter kinda smilin' and noddin' every time ol' Charles got thumped. Finally, Jean says, "*I'm calling the sheriff*," and we let her do it.

There isn't any regular police force in town, so it took ten or fifteen minutes for Deputy Bill to show up. By that time, ol' Charlie looked like he'd been up all night sortin' bobcats, and you never saw anybody so pleased to see a cop.

But I'll give Charlie credit. As he was bein' led away, Georgie said, "Charles, how could you swindle women who trusted you?"

Charlie slowly shook his head and said, "Well, Georgie, I can't swindle women who don't."

"When I was drivin' in this morning," Luther said, "I found myself behind a car driven by a woman who was talkin' to her female passenger. When we got to the traffic light, it was red. They stopped and sat there talkin' through red ... and green ... and yellow and red.

"Finally, I got out, walked up to the car and rapped on the window. She rolled it down. "Lady," I said, "this light only comes in three colors. If you don't have a favorite outta them three, you'll just have to choose from what's available."

Luther took a slug of coffee. "Damn near ran over my foot," he said indignantly.

Pete was down to the Capitol a while back, and he came back really impressed by all the magnificent buildings, tall statues and sculptured lawns.

"It's quite a place," Pete reported. "Jesus would have been born there if God could've only located three wise men and a virgin."

I was asking Tom about his boy the other day. The kid's been at the University for quite a while now and can't seem to make up his mind about what he wants to do for a living.

"Oh, he's doing fine," Tom said. "I can't say the same for the guy, (that would me me), who has to foot the bill."

"Don't tell me he's changed his major again?" I asked.

"Yep."

"What's he going to be now?"

"A politician."

Well as you know, I think politicians are, for the most part, bottomfeeders, and I have no use for them. But I tried not to let it show and said, "So he's majoring in political science, eh?"

"No," growled Tom, "but anybody who's become this good at spending other people's money is bound to wind up a politician."

Old Bill Richey was a good man, and he made his fortune by workin' harder than most folks and takin' a risk if the odds seemed favorable.

His daughters, though, grew up thinkin' that money and class are the same thing. They think of themselves as the creme de la creme (to you and me that's the scum on top) of our local society.

Now old Bill used to start off every day with a shot of good bourbon, and he'd end it the same way. None of the daughters cared much for their father's drinking or his habit of hangin' around with "common laborers" as the daughters liked to call people who worked for a living. Juliette, especially was scandalized by the whole thing.

After high school, Juliette went off to one of those fancy private colleges. Four years later she graduated and showed up with her fiancee. He was one of those slick, arrogant kids that you might expect Juliette to light on. Well, the kid being a high society type just couldn't see his way past her father.

Bill owned thousands of acres of land, a farm machinery company, most of a bank, and a blue serge suit. I can vouch for the suit, 'cause I saw him wear it once. He had a blue silk tie that went with it that was prob'ly eight or ten inches wide. The kid called off the marriage and left.

Now, Morton's a nice guy, and I've known him for years. His father owned a second-hand store and junkyard, and Morton was learning the business. Nobody could figure out how he managed the time to romance Juliette since Morton spent his spare time holding up one end of

Jensen's bar with the able assistance of his buddy, Cecil Burdette. Strangest of all, the marriage worked. Not real well most of the time, but it worked. They had an anniversary celebration not long ago, and Martha and I were invited ... by Morton.

We finally decided to go because we knew Juliette would be inviting all her friends from down at the state capitol, and Morton would be kind of on his own. But when we got there, we found out Morton had more friends than we thought. The party had split up. On one side were the shot-and-a-beer crowd, and on the other were evening clothes and tall glasses with little umbrellas stickin' out. Believe it or not, things went pretty well up until Cecil belched.

You see, when Cecil Burdette burps, he makes no secret of it. Everybody for a quarter of a mile knows about it. Juliette sure knew. She marched up to Cecil and called him an "uncouth, drunken lout," and said, "Why don't you go back to the grog shop where you belong?"

Cecil straightened himself up and looked down on her. "Jul-ee-ette," he said. "I've heard that high society folks have bathrooms in their houses, but that they're for guests only. I've heard that when you've reached a certain station in life, then you're beyond all that and don't use the bathroom yourself. And just between us, as tight as you're wired, I can believe it."

Juliette really ripped into him then, and Morton stepped in to defend his friend. That's when the real argument started. Morton was pretty loaded and was getting the worst of it when Juliette yelled, "I was a fool when I married you!"

Morton weaved a little, burped, and said, "You're right, but I was drunk at the time, and didn't notice."

Martha and I went home. The next day Morton was at the cafe having coffee when Cecil came in. "I just want to tell you," Morton said, "that I really appreciate you're staying until the end of the party, expecially after what Juliette said to you."

"What kind of friend would I be if I did that?" said Cecil. "All of us, at least all of us on that side of the room, are your friends. It would be impolite to leave. I just waited around until I was carried out with everybody else."

Sometimes when I hire these college kids, it's their first real job and some of 'em are amazed to find out that work is involved.

A case in point would be a young lady named Violet. She usually got here late, went home early, and when she was here, you had to drive a stake and take a sight on her to see if she was actually movin'.

"What happened to Violet?" Joe asked a few

weeks ago. "I haven't seen her around lately."

"I had to let her go," I answered.

"Well, that's too bad. So now you have a vacancy."

"Not really. Violet didn't leave a vacany."

Luther was married briefly when he was young, and I asked him if it had made him a confirmed bachelor.

"Oh, no," he said. "For quite a while there I thought I'd prob'ly get married again."

"Why didn't you," I replied.

"Well, I figured there was no hurry. There's lots of fish in the sea."

"So, what happened?"

Luther took a swig of coffee, shook his head and grinned. "The bait got too old."

I don't know if you've been in Jensen's tavern, but it looks a lot better since Jack took it over from his dad. Old Ralph started out fine, but things gradually went downhill over the years. In the beginning, there were booths along the walls, a semi-circular bar with stools, a sign posted on the back wall that said, *CUSTOMERS ARE EXPECTED TO CARRY OUT THEIR OWN DEAD*; and a juke box with room for dancing. In the back there were a couple of pool tables and a shuffleboard with a card room beyond that. He did a good business.

After a while, Jensen decided to offer a hot lunch to his customers and installed a hamburger grill. But before the health department would let him use it, they required he put in a hood over the grill to vent the grease and smoke.

Jensen was outraged. He tried every way he could to get around the requirement, but those health department boys wouldn't budge. Maybe it was that contest of wills between two parties (which was true enough) or just that Jensen was a lousy carpenter (also true) or maybe he was too cheap to spend money on something he thought unnecessary ... but the fact is he finally broke down and installed the hood and vent pipe.

I guess the health department boys were tired of fightin' with him and didn't look too close when it was done. All I know is that if you leaned over the grill and looked up into the hood, you could see a good sized patch of blue sky.

Well, things went pretty well that summer and some folks did try a hamburger - always served with a handful of potato chips - at Jensen's Tavern and Grill. Of course, the new sign he had put up cost more than he was ever goin' to make selling burgers, but by now it was the principle of the thing. We're not even goin' to discuss the cost of the grill and the fancy open-to-the-atmosphere hood.

Anyhow, as with most things he did, Jensen gradually lost interest when the "new" wore off. Most of his customers were locals anyway. Jensen's Tavern was where farmers and ranchers met to talk livestock and crop prices and enjoy a beer. The wives got together to find out how all the other folks around the country were gettin' on while the kids climbed the trees out back or played in the crick (not creek, crick) that ran behind the tavern. Most people ate at home in those days, and when they did go out to eat, it was usually for a real sit-down meal. Not that Jensen himself didn't have something to do with the decline in his hamburger business. He had a lot to do with it.

Not to get down on him, you understand, but the fact is I never saw Jensen when he was clean shaven ... he always seemed to have a three-day growth of beard. Somewhere he must have found a place that sold flannel shirts that came with holes in the elbows, brand new, because I don't think he even owned a shirt that had a complete sleeve. He always wore old gray or tan pants (with at least one knobby knee peekin' through) and old, runover, black oxfords -- no socks. He completed his ensemble with an ancient, sweat-stained, gray felt hat that I never saw him without. It had a hole, too, at the top of the crown where you'd naturally put your hand to put it on or take it off -- so I'm guessing he didn't sleep with it.

What I'm sayin' is ... his personal habits didn't lend themselves to folks droolin' at the thought of one of his hamburgers.

Anyway, like I said, things went along pretty well until fall when the rains came and the grill started to rust. It rusted all winter and, according to Jensen, mighta been ruined except that come spring a couple of pigeons nested in the vent pipe and blocked off the moisture. Well, most of the moisture.

It was about that same time that Milton Hewitt complained that his glass of draft beer was darker than usual. Jensen inspected things and determined this was probably due to the cigar stub in the bottom of the glass. Just to show that he valued his regular customers, he poured the whole thing out and fished out the cigar butt before he refilled the glass.

But as Jensen later observed, "Times change and so do peoples' tastes and the wide-awake businessman keeps up with stuff like that. I'm droppin' my draft line. Folks only want bottled or canned beer these days."

As the years went by, the felt got ripped on the pool tables and balls were either lost or beaten out of shape. The card table had a broken leg, and it was propped up by three or four cases of empty beer bottles. The shuffleboard was still in working order, but its surface was sticky with dried beer and soda pop, and if you wanted to use it, you

had to move the ten or fifteen cases of empties stacked on top of it. For that matter, there wasn't a flat surface in the joint with the exception of the bar itself that didn't have cases of dead soldiers sitting on it.

I was just a kid, but I recall being in Jensen's buyin' a soda pop, I guess, when a stranger walked in. You didn't see a suit and tie very often around our part of the country, but this guy had both. He had an attitude, too.

"Gimme a beer," he growled, as he sat on a bar stool. I'd guess he was about six feet tall, skinny, and in his mid-twenties. Maybe he was havin' a bad day, but that didn't mean he had to bring it in and leave it with us.

"What brand?" Jensen asked.

"I don't care what brand," the man snapped. "Just get a beer in front of me right now."

Jensen only had one gait, and he didn't plan on gettin' into a trot for nobody, even if they were some kind of hotshot. By the time he placed the bottle in front of the customer, the guy was sayin' "take your time, why don't you?" Jensen just held out his hand and replied, "Forty cents."

While the guy was reaching in his pocket, he said, "gimme a burger, too. How much is that altogether?"

"A hamburger?"

"Yes, a hamburger," the man snarled. "That's what the sign outside reads. Tavern and Grill! or can't any of you hicks in this town read? And snap it up. I'm in a hurry."

"A dollar fifty, total," said Jensen.

Well, when Jensen had been sellin' hamburgers a few years back, he only charged sixty cents. We all knew right off it was his way of gettin' back at this fella for bein' so ornery. When I say WE, I mean Frank Peagram and Milton Hewitt besides myself. When I saw Frank and Milt exchange smiles, I thought I knew what it meant, Jensen raisin' his price and all. But, like most kids, I hadn't looked far enough ahead.

With a heavy sigh, Jensen turned around and stared at the cases of empties stacked behind the bar. Then he started moving them, stacking them wherever he could until the grill became visible. On the grill itself were a few discarded cigarette cartons, a claw hammer, screwdriver, pliers and a half-rotted old bar rag. These were also put aside except the hammer, and it was placed next to the grill.

Jensen turned the switch and got things to heatin' up. Frank and Milt, I noticed were watching the stranger whose face looked like mine probably did when I stepped in something warm and squishy -- barefooted.

Anyhow, next to the cooler Jensen had one of these old freezers, with four lids on top that either folded back or lifted clear off. He lifted off one set, stuck his head down in there and rooted around for a while. When he straightened up he had a hunk of frost in his hand about the size of your head. Then he sat it on the corner of the freezer and went to whalin' away at it with the hammer. After he'd knocked off three or four pounds of frost, it turned out to be a stack of hamburger patties. They were pretty pale and frost-burned, but they were hamburger patties, sure enough. Jensen used the claw on the hammer to pry one loose.

I looked over at that arrogant city feller and his mouth was movin' but nothin' was comin' out.

The grill had a kind of grease pot hooked on its side, and there was handle stickin' out of it. Jensen took hold of the pot, grabbed the handle and went to pullin' and tuggin' at it. After a while, it came loose along with a big glob of grease that was kind of a rosy color with big black chunks in it. When he scraped the grease off on the side of the pot, it turned out he was holding a spatula. The grill was covered in rust, dust, grease, grass and a few other things that pigeons nesting in the flue had let drop, so to speak. Jensen went to scrapin' at it with the spatula.

I heard a little whimperin' sound and turned to look at the stranger. He was all pasty-faced, and even though I was just a kid, he didn't look like a well man to me.

Jensen finished his job and stood leaning over

the grill with his hands on each side, one holding the spatula and the other a petrified patty, while he waited for the grill to get hot. After a while, he tested the surface by sticking a finger in his mouth and tapping it, but it didn't sizzle.

"Not yet," he muttered. After a minute or so, when he was just puckering up again, there came the roar of a motor and the sound of car tires diggin' out in the gravel. Jensen turned to look at us. "Where'd he go?"

"Beats me," said Frank. "He just up and left."

"Well," replied Jensen, and you could tell he was really offended. "How do you like that? Go out of your way for somebody, give 'em personal service, and they run out on you. It's a good thing I made him pay up front." He turned to look at me. "Let that be a lesson to you, Bud. Just because a fella wears a suit and tie don't make him somethin' special. He had no class. I could tell that right off."

"Well said," nodded Frank.

"I got stuck in traffic behind Mildred Tibbs yesterday," Luther was saying, "so it gave me plenty of time to think."

"Don't I know it," added Pete. "That ol' DeSoto of hers ain't seen forty miles an hour in its life."

"Well," Luther went on, "I got to thinkin'

45

about how my mother used to tell me I should always wear clean underwear, especially if I was travelin'. That way, if I was in an accident and got taken to the hospital, the people there wouldn't think poorly of me."

"Everybody's mother says that," put in Tom.

"Exactly," Luther nodded, "and I got to thinkin' about young Warren Teal and how he goes rippin' around in that car of his. You gotta know it's only a matter of time before he ends up in the hospital. I'll bet he wears clean underwear every day."

"So what's all this mean?" I asked, not sure I really wanted to know.

"As I see it," Luther went on, "there's only one possible explanation. Mildred Tibbs hasn't changed her underwear since the Truman administration."

Tom mentioned the other day that his youngest son was home for a few days. I asked how Brad was gettin' along in school.

"Good," nodded Tom. "So good, in fact, I believe he's thinking of turning professional. He told me he'd changed his major again. That's four or five times now. Says he's trying to find himself. I told him he's looking in the wrong place. If he'd just stop by a barber shop, I'd be willing to bet that they'd find him under there somewhere."

Tom grinned and took a sip of coffee. "I guess I shouldn't complain. He doesn't wear earrings. Well, with the length of his hair, I have to take his word for it. Hell, I have to take his word that he's wearing a shirt."

"Quit kickin' about it," I said. "Be glad that you don't have to take his word that he's wearin' pants."

"My Uncle Willy buckarooed all over the high desert country for eight or ten years." Pete explained. "But he got tired of workin' for other folks and decided to go into business for himself. The Depression had kicked in not long before and times were tough for everybody, cattlemen included. Why, at one time, jack rabbits were known far and wide as 'Hoover hogs.' But Willy was a good manager, so he said, and he thought he could pull it off.

"He found him a little rawhide outfit somewhere out there forty miles back of beyond and bought the feller out for little or nothin'. A couple of dozen scrawny old range cows came with the place along with a gimpy old one-eyed bull that was prob'ly a calf when Taft was elected.

"The first thing he did was ride around and meet his new neighbors. 'Course he knew 'em already, had even worked for a few of 'em and was well liked by everybody.

"Well, Willy went to work in his new business, and turned out to be a fine rancher. Why that next year all his cows had twin calves, and that little herd was really on the increase. The next year he managed those cows so well that the ones that didn't give birth to triplets had four or five calves before the year was out. Folks around that part of the country said they'd never seen the like. Naturally, they admired him no end.

"Cattle ranchers are generally pretty friendly folks anyhow, and considerate of their neighbors, but there were a few of the locals that seemed to be gettin' a little jealous of Willy's success. The following year Willy's cows not only had litters of calves, but his yearlings did as well. Why even the bull had a calf or two.

"Those jealous fellers didn't like to see somebody do so well, especially since their own poor management has caused a noticeable decrease in their herds the last two or three years. One or two even got downright uncivil towards ol' Willy.

"The next year my Uncle Bert rode into that country to visit Willy, but the ranch was deserted ... not a man or critter to be found anywhere ... and it looked like there hadn't been for some time. Bert rode around to several of the local ranches to ask after Willy.

"The story was all pretty much the same. Shortly after the fall roundup, Willy took sick. It came on sudden, folks said, and had something to do with his breathing. Some people thought that the desert air contributed to it, and suggested to Willy that a change of location would be good for his health. Willy shied at the idea, of course, but a bunch of his friends got together and rode over to see him one day.

"They said Willy's condition was downright shocking. They all agreed that something had to be done. Speakin' to him, as friends will, they told him they greatly feared for his health and, from the looks of him, they'd bet to the last man that if Willy didn't find a more genial climate, he'd be dead by the end of the week. They told Bert they all missed ol' Willy, but it was for the best."

"Y'know," says Luther, "I'm gettin' mighty tired of payin' doctors and lawyers to 'practice'. For that kind of money I think I've got a right to expect the real thing."

Ernie Kern, was a local farmer and pretty well off. To say he was frugal would be putting it mildly. Anyhow, one day Ernie runs across Jake Barker. Jake was a farmer, too, but money was a scarce thing with him, and he just had to make do as best he could.

"Say, Jake," Ernie says, "I've got a mule that has pin worms. I'd call out the vet but he charges too much. You got any home remedies?"

"Well," Jake replies, "I had a mule that had pin worms. I just poured a quart of turpentine down him."

A month or so later Ernie happens to meet Jake again.

"Y'know that mule I was telling you about?" Ernie says. "The one that had the pin worms? Well, I poured a quart of turpentine down him and he died."

Jake just nodded. "Yeah," he said, "so did mine."

Bud's can't fail diet
1. List all the things you like to eat.
2. Don't eat 'em.

"Funny how a kid will get strange ideas," Pete was sayin'. "When I was a little feller all the men around that I saw were clean shaven. I got to lookin' at comics and magazines and whatnot, and I somehow got the idea that those bushy sideburns that the old timers wore came from hair growin' out of their ears. On top of that, I thought that the

big ol' handlebar mustaches must be hair growin' out of their noses. Later on, though, I came to understand otherwise.

"But y'know," he said, leanin' forward with a shake of his head, "now that I'm gettin' a little long in the tooth myself and at the rate I've got hair growin' out of those two places, I'm beginnin' to think maybe I was right in the first place."

DO YOU REMEMBER

Playing baseball until it was too dark to see the ball? Wax lips and mustaches? Speaking of wax do you recall those little wax "pop bottles" you'd buy for a penny? You'd bite off the cap and suck out the sweet syrup inside. Then you'd chew the wax.

Did you have a metal lunch box? What kind? Roy Rogers? Flash Gordon? The Cisco Kid and Pancho with their horses, Diablo and Loco?

When you walked home from school did you cut across the pasture while keeping an eye out for the bull? Remember that time you didn't see the bull, and he spotted you half-way across? You had to run like crazy for the fence and, when you got there, throw your lunch box over while you dived under ... and the thermos broke ... and Mom was mad about it ... and you didn't dare tell her how it happened.

Remember when the family went on a two-week vacation, and nobody could recall seeing the house key for at least a year? It wasn't necessary to look for the car keys, though. They were where they always were - in the ignition. When you filled up the car with gas, you got a free glass or piece of flatware.

There was that boy in school who wore those big ol' work boots, and the girl who made penmanship an art form.

Did you sit in the living room staring at the light and trying to stay awake so you could hear "Gunsmoke" on the radio? Or Jack Benny, or Amos n' Andy or The Shadow? Remember when Fibber McGee opened the closet? What about that creepy creaking door that opened with each segment of Inner Sanctum?

There was that chewing gum that came in a little cardboard box. The gum was in little white candy-coated squares. And one day you were poking around in the medicine cabinet (which was strictly off limits) and discovered a chewing gum laxative that looked just like the regular gum. The next day the mean kid spent a little of his time in class with his hand up and the rest of it in the bathroom. And you knew there'd be a fight if he ever figured it out.

There was that clock on the classroom wall that the janitor wound once a week. And time inched along ever so slowly until -- freedom! Bikes with big tires and red wagons when the weather was good. Snow forts and sleds in the winter.

Nobody wanted to get sent to the principal's office. Sure, it wasn't pleasant, but it wouldn't make a freckle on the face of an outraged parent ... you were gonna pay ... big time.

The Saturday matinee with Gene Autry and Champion. It was always preceded by a serial that closed with Batman or the Durango Kid clinging to the edge of a cliff by their fingernails as the villain approached with a sneer ... "Don't miss next week's exciting installment of ..."

Y'know, maybe we've been trying the wrong approach to solving the problems of the world. Maybe we should all just get together and have one helluva big pillow fight.

"It's been quite a few years ago now," Joe was sayin' not long ago, "but I guess you recall when Mynah birds were the newest craze in pets. Well, Marge and I were in the city one day, and she wanted to stop by a pet store she knew about that had one of these critters. When we walked in, there was a gray haired, distinguished looking fella walking out.

"Marge spoke to the owner, who was behind the counter, and the guy nodded at the gray haired fella who was getting into his car in the parking lot."

"*I know you're here to see the mynah bird*, the owner said. *I thought the Reverend Melcher there was gonna buy him. He spent over an our back there with that bird.*

"We walked to the back of the store and, sure enough, there was this ugly little feathered beast that looked kinda like a starling. The store owner had followed us to the back.

"He walked up to the cage and shook his head. *Well, Major*, he said, *I thought sure you were gonna have a new owner. I wonder why the Reverend didn't buy you.*

"Major hopped from one perch to another, cocked his head, and stared out at us. *You're a nice bird*, he said, *but you're too damned expensive.*"

When old Pat Deeley won the state lottery a while back he was interviewed by a reporter.

"What do you plan to do with all that money?" the reporter asked.

Pat took off his hat, scratched his head, and squinted his eyes into the future. "Well," says Pat, "I been a farmer my whole life. Don't know nothin' else. So," he said with a sigh, "I guess I'll just keep on farmin' til it's all gone."

Luther, as you know, was divorced as a young man and never remarried. It's safe to say his Christmas list isn't exactly overcrowded with attorneys. Anyhow, I'm standin' at the door the other morning when he drives up. Now, his old pickup isn't what you'd call a thing of beauty in the first place, but I notice it's got a couple of new dents and has a good coating of dirt, grass, leaves and twigs clear up on the hood.

"Luther," I say as he gets out and walks past me, "what happened to your pickup?"

Luther raises an eyebrow. "What? Oh, yeah. I ran over a lawyer."

"Really," I say. "Well, that explains the dents, but what about all the leaves 'n grass 'n stuff?"

Luther takes his cup from the shelf and heads for the coffee pot. "Missed him the first time," he says, "An' he took to the woods."

Guerilla shopping: our wives at holiday sales.

Tom was back on his movies kick the other morning. "They're cutting back on violence," he says, "so you see the hero packin' around a pistol big enough to derail a locomotive or else it holds enough ammo to supply a small army.

"And so he gets into it with the bad guy and what's the first thing he does? Right, he loses it. Now he has to go up against the bad guy barehanded.

"The bad guy, of course, is set to slice open the hero's gizzard and what's he got? A chain saw, an ax, two or three swords and body odor.

"Of course, they beat each other to a bloody pulp before the hero wins. But you gotta admit nobody got killed.

"Another thing," he says, taking a swig of coffee. "There's a woman running from a monster. Let's say it's a giant slug with six inch fangs (dripping blood, naturally), and it leaves a slime trail three feet wide as it moves along at maybe half a mile an hour.

"Can this woman outrun it? Nope. It's gaining on her. What does she do? Right. She trips and falls down. If she's alone, she trips three or four times. Do monsters only attack clumsy people or what? And if there's a guy with her? She says *'Oh, I think I've twisted my ankle.'* Apparently twisting an ankle paralyzes her entire body. She can't move!"

Tom puts down his cup and looks sour.

"Listen," he says, "if I twist my ankle and there's a slime monster about to stick his fangs in my carcass, you're gonna see a one-legged man setting some speed records while he hauls his butt outta there."

Pete and Gladys got into it again. He was tellin' me about it and I said, "Well, Pete, Gladys has always been outspoken."

"Oh yeah?" he fires back. "Not by anybody I know."

LeRoy was sittin' on a bench out front when Mildred Tibbs jumped his case.

"LeRoy," she says, "why don't you get a job? Go to work."

"Why?"

"So you could put something away for retirement. So you could relax in your golden years and not have to work."

"I ain't workin' now," says LeRoy.

Elmer wobbled into Doc Guthrie's office for a checkup. Afterwards he says, "Well, Doc, how do I stand?"

"Elmer," she replies, "It beats the hell outta me."

Deputy Bill, our local county mountie, stops in sometimes for coffee if he's been workin' the late shift. The other morning he's tellin' us about an older couple he pulled over.

"I walk up to the car and ask for the guy's license," Bill says. "*You were goin' kinda fast*, I tell him."

"The wife, sitting on the far side yells, *What'd he say?*

"The guy looks over at her. *Says we were speeding.*

"I'm looking at the guy's license and remark, *I see you're from the state capitol.*

"*What'd he say?* yells the wife.

"The guy looks over at her. *Says we're from the capitol.*

"I shake my head and say, *The orneriest, stubbornest, most hard-to-get-along-with woman I ever met was in that town.*

"*What'd he say?* yells the wife.

"The guy looks over at her. *Says he thinks he knows you.*"

I'm not saying Bud's coffee is strong," says Tom, "but it's a known fact that on a Monday, old Ed Wilkins came in here and had a cup, died on Tuesday and by Thursday, Creedy, the undertaker, was still trying to get him to hold still long enough to get his suit on him."

We were all still half asleep the other morning, and it was quiet around the table when Joe ups and says, "Ain't nothin' worse than a ree-formed."

"Ree-formed what?" asks Luther.

"Don't matter," Joe replies. "Ree-formed drinker, smoker, overeater or sinner. If they're ree-formed, they're a pain."

Like any small town, we have our share of eccentrics. There are several people around here who mind their own business.

Ol' Zeke turned 97 not long ago. "Zeke," I said, "how does a man get to be 97 years old?"

"Well, first off," Zeke replies, "is make sure you was born 97 years ago."

You were a black businessman who had to wait a half-hour for a connecting flight in a little out-of-the-way airport. You walked into the bar and saw the lone patron was a young soldier. Taking the stool next to him, you ordered a drink, loosened your tie, and tried to strike up a conversation.

The soldier wouldn't say much, and about all you could get him to tell you was that he was fresh from a combat zone and trying to get home. For the next half-hour you carried the conversation while the soldier nodded and swirled the drink in his glass.

He didn't mention that an hour before he'd been seated next to a woman whose son was about to be sent to that same combat zone. In her mind, the fact that this soldier should come back alive cut down the chances that her son would, too, and she was outraged.

He didn't tell you about the firefight less than three days ago, and he wouldn't or couldn't talk about his plane landing in the United States: about the war protesters screaming filthy names, throwing bottles and garbage ... and worse. A first and lasting impression: "Soldier, you have no home. The country of your birth loathes you."

Your flight was called. You bought the young soldier a drink, shook his hand and said, "Welcome home."

It would be many, many years later, when veterans of another war were being welcomed home, before he would hear those words again. Once from a TV newswoman, who didn't mean it, and once from a young auto mechanic, who did.

So whoever you are and wherever you may be ... you have been remembered fondly and often over the years. May the road rise up to meet you.